INVASION of the BODY SNATCHERS
FILM LOCATIONS

There was something wrong in Santa Mira!

INVASION of the BODY SNATCHERS FILM LOCATIONS

by Jerry L. Schneider

Invasion of the Body Snatchers
Film Locations

Copyright 2009-2025 by Jerry L. Schneider

All rights reserved. No part of this book may be reproduced or transmitted in any form by any means, electronic, mechanical, photocopying, recording, or by any information source and retrieval system now known or to be invented, without prior written permission of the publisher, except for the quoting of brief passages in connection with a review of this book.

Some material herein, previously copyrighted, is in the Public Domain in the United States of America. Some quotes may be protected by copyright and are used in this reference/research work under the "Fair Use Doctrine" of the U. S. Copyright Law.

First Edition published 2009
Enlarged and Expanded Second Edition published March 2025

ISBN 979-8-9900581-3-2

Published by
CP Entertainment Books
www.cpentbooks.com

INVASION of the BODY SNATCHERS
FILM LOCATIONS

THE CAST AND THEIR ROLES

Kevin McCarthy	.....	Dr. Miles J. Bennell
Dana Wynter	.....	Becky Driscoll
Larry Gates	.....	Dr. Danny Kauffman
King Donovan	.....	Jack Belicec
Carolyn Jones	.....	Teddy Belicec
Jean Willes	.....	Nurse Sally Withers
Ralph Dumke	.....	Officer Nick Miller
Virginia Christine	.....	Wilma Lentz
Tom Fadden	.....	Ira Lentz
Kenneth Patterson	.....	Stanley Driscoll
Guy Way	.....	Officer Sam Janzek
Eileen Stevens	.....	Anne Grimaldi
Beatrice Maude	.....	Grandma Grimaldi
Jean Andren	.....	Eleda Lentz
Bobby Clark	.....	Jimmy Grimaldi
Everett Glass	.....	Dr. Ed Pursey
Dabbs Greer	.....	Mac Lomax
Pat O'Malley	.....	Baggage Man
Guy Renie	.....	Restaurant Owner
Marie Selland	.....	Martha Lomax
Sam Peckinpah	.....	Charlie Buckholtz
Harry J. Vejar	.....	Pod Carrier in Miles' Office
Whit Bissell	.....	Dr. Hill
Richard Deacon	.....	Dr. Harvey Bassett
Frank Hagney	.....	Bit part
Robert Osterloh	.....	Ambulance Driver

THE LOCATIONS

The Hospital	...	Allied Artists Studio
Santa Mira Train Depot	...	Chatsworth Train Depot
Grimaldi's Vegetable Stand	...	Lassen Street west of Mason Ave., Chatsworth
Dr. Bennell's Office Interior	...	Allied Artists Studio
Wilma Lentz' Home	...	1635 Rancho Ave., Glendale
Sky Terrace	...	Woodland Hills Country Club, 21150 Dumetz Rd, Woodland Hills
Belicec Home Exterior	...	Chandler Estate, 2411 Inverness Ave.
Belicec Home Interior	...	Allied Artists Studio
Becky Driscoll's Home	...	1927 Rodney Dr.
Wilma Lentz's Store	...	20 S. Baldwin Ave., Sierra Madre
Lomax Gas Station	...	1200 N. Virgil Ave.
Alley near Lomax Gas Station	...	½ block west of Lomax location, south of Lexington Ave.
Sally Wither's House	...	4400 Russell St.
Alley & Stairs behind Bennell's Office	...	Alley east of Vermont Ave, behind the 1710 block
Santa Mira Town Center	...	Sierra Madre Town Center
Front Exterior to Bennell's Office	...	26 W. Sierra Madre Blvd., Sierra Madre
The Chase	...	Begins at intersection of Beachwood Dr., Belden Dr., and Westshire Dr.
The Stairs	...	Bottom between 2744-2748 Westshire Dr., top between 2823-2831 Hollyridge Dr.
Bronson Canyon	...	North end of Canyon Dr.
Pod Farm	...	600 Wilcox Ave., Sierra Madre
The Final Exterior Scenes	...	Mulholland Dr. & Hollywood Freeway (101)

INVASION of the BODY SNATCHERS
FILM LOCATIONS

THE HOSPITAL

"Will you let me go while there's still time?"

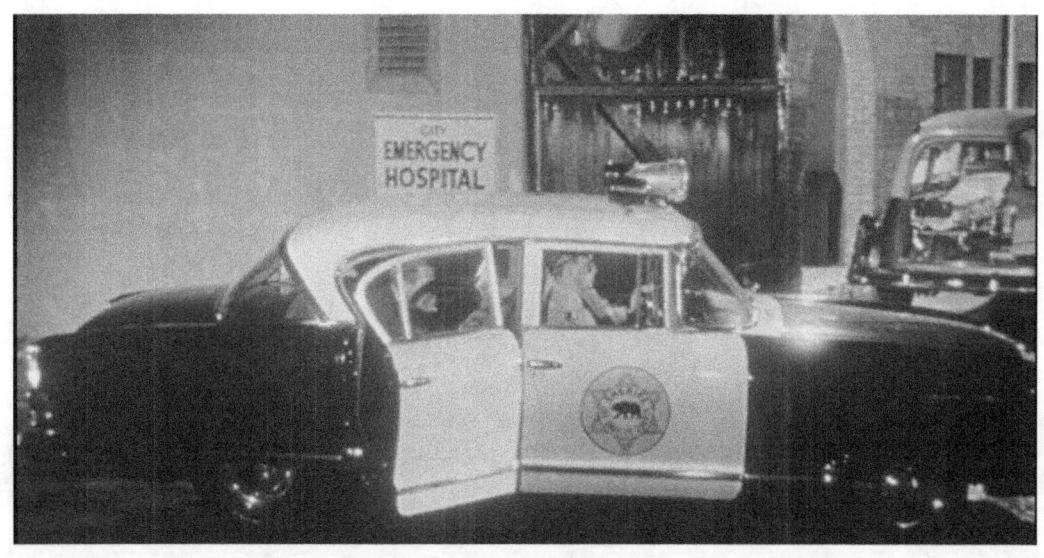

"Doctor, will you tell these fools I'm not crazy!
Make them listen to me before it's too late!"

The beginning of the film used the Monogram/Allied Artists Studio west exterior located on North Commonwealth Ave. That street has now been closed and is on the old studio property now owned by Scientology. Below are more current views of this side of the studio.

Facing Page Bottom: A current aerial view, looking east at the prior N. Commonwealth Avenue side of the current studio location. **Below:** A current aerial view showing the 3 sound stages. A white arrow shows the location of the entrance used for the hospital. **Bottom:** A Sanborn Fire Insurance Map of the studio property and surrounding neighborhood. The studio, at that time, was bounded by Hoover on the east, Commonwealth on the west, Sunset Drive on the north, and houses on the south.

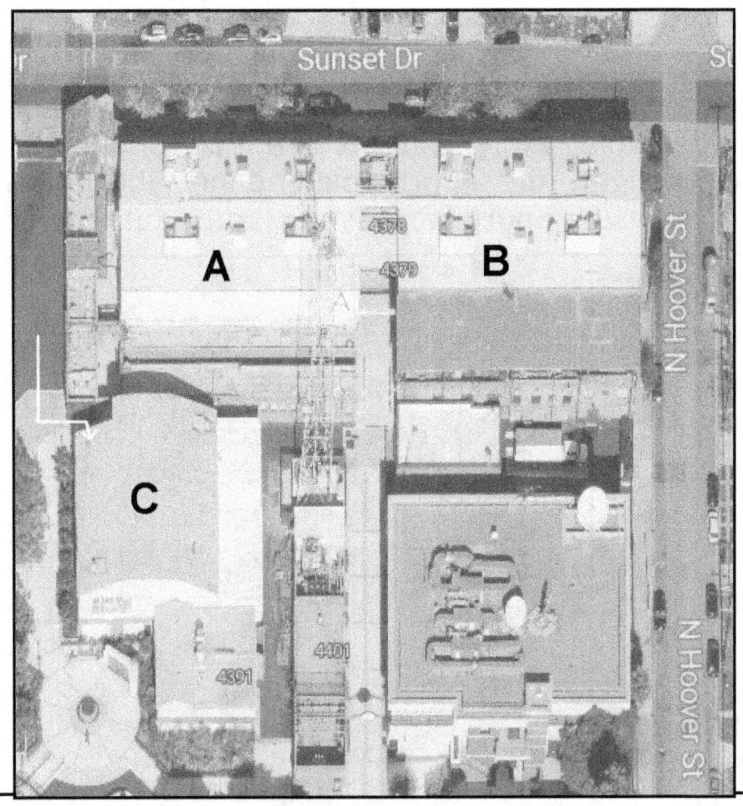

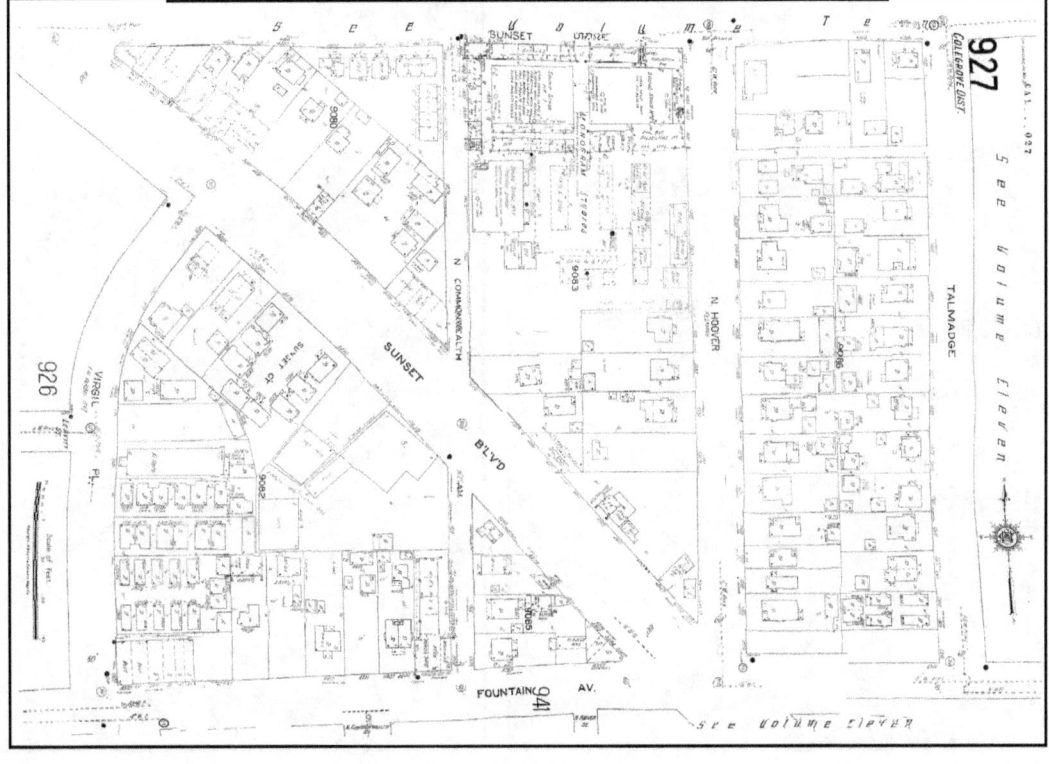

SANTA MIRA RAILROAD STATION

The Santa Mira railroad station scenes were filmed at the old Chatsworth Train Depot. The depot is long gone. It was located just east of Remmet Avenue, north of Dupont Street, and west of the train tracks. This location is now almost due west (slightly north) of the current Chatsworth Metrolink Station, which is located on the east side of the train tracks near the intersection of Mayall Street and Old Depot Plaza Road.

On the vintage aerial photograph below left, the depot location is shown in the black circle. The road leading away from the depot is in the black rectangle. On the modern aerial below right, the approximate depot location is a small white rectangle and the road leading northward is the large white rectangle.

*"I hurried home from the medical convention I had been attending.
At first glance everything looked the same. It wasn't.
Something evil had taken possession of the town."*

This now shot was taken from the east side of the tracks, just north of the Metrolink station. On the opposite side of the tracks was the location of the depot in the film and where the buildings on the left side of the tracks is where one of the dirt roads led away from the depot..

The Chatsworth Train Depot in the 1950's.

"Wally Eberhard was in twice and called three times about something, but he wouldn't tell me what it was."

GRIMALDI'S VEGETABLE STAND

*"The boy's panic should have told me
that it was more than school he was afraid of."*

*"And that littered, closed-up vegetable stand should have told me something, too.
When I last saw it less than a month ago, it was the cleanest and busiest stand
on the road.""*

The Grimaldi's Vegetable Stand was located in Chatsworth on Lassen Street, west of Mason Avenue. In the aerial below, the vegetable stand is shown in the black circle.

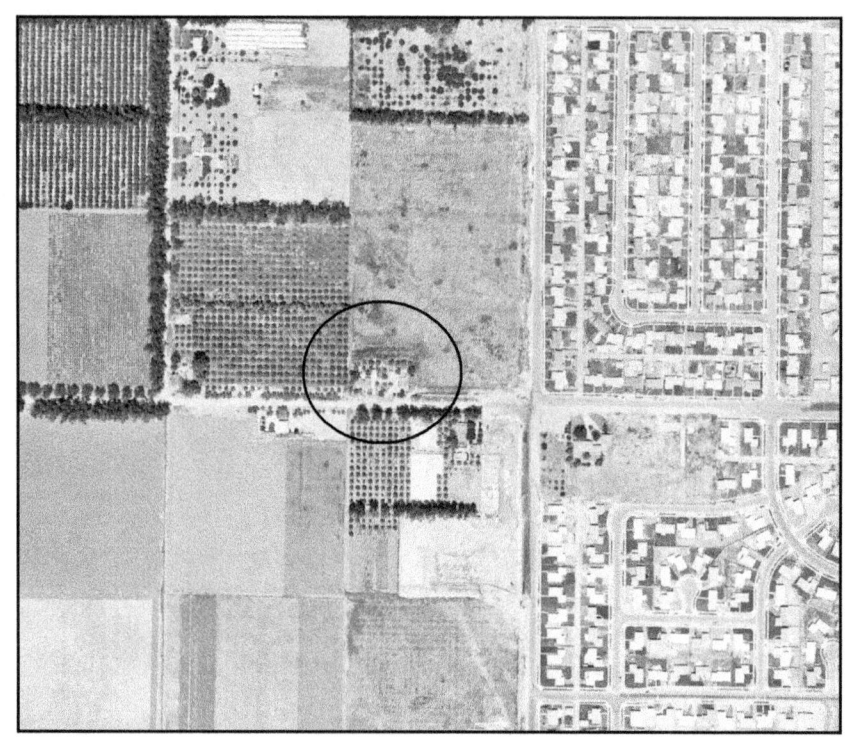

DR. MILES BENNELL'S DOCTOR'S OFFICE

"I've been in Reno. Dad tells me you were there too."

"Well, I guess that makes us lodge brothers now. Except that I'm paying dues while you collect them."

Dr. Miles Bennell's doctor office was located in a professional/medical building, on the second floor, at 1710 N. Vermont Avenue, on the east side of the street, between Kingswell Avenue on the north and Prospect Avenue on the south.

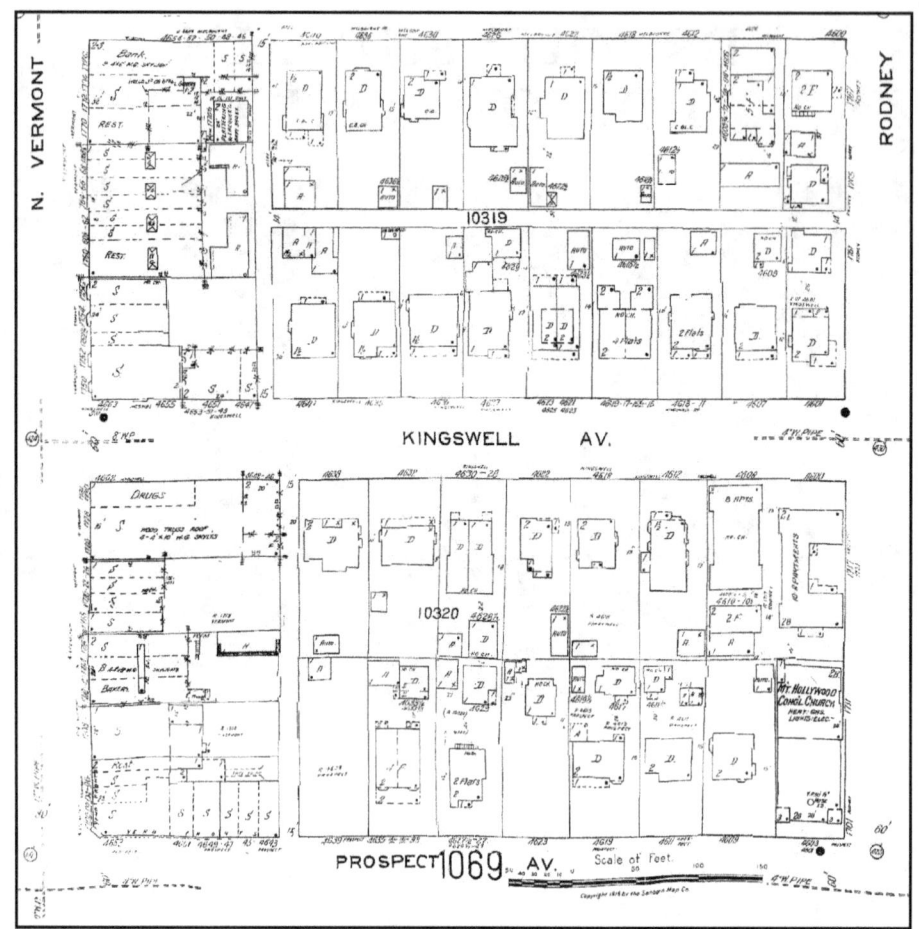

The above partial view of a Sanborn Fire Insurance Map shows 1710 N. Vermont Avenue on the lower left portion, identified as "Bakery". The bakery was on the ground floor of the building. The offices and at least one apartment were located on the second floor. Below is an aerial view of the same location. The left/right rectangle is the location of the building while the top/bottom rectangle is the parking lot where Dr. Bennell and Becky Driscoll parked while on the run.

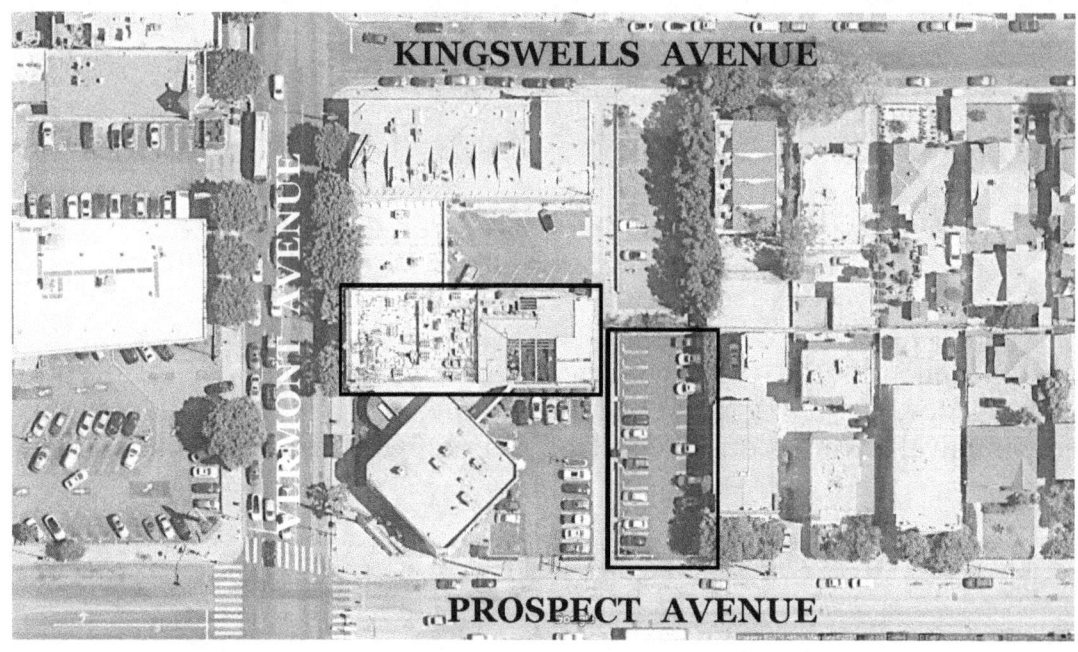

The exterior of Dr. Miles Bennell's office was located in Sierra Madre on the south side of Sierra Madre Boulevard, west of Baldwin Avenue, and just west of the end of Kirsting Court. Those three streets make up the triangular park area and is the center of the town of Sierra Madre and Santa Mira. The front of the building housed businesses, but the rear was the Sierra Madre Hotel. While the building is still intact, the hotel portion is now gone as well as the street exit.

"My nurse tells me you were in last week and wanted very much to see me."
"It wasn't anything important."

12

WILMA LENTZ'S HOME

"Nice to see you, Wilma." "Let's have it. You talked to him. What do you think?"
"It's him. He's your uncle Ira, all right."

"HE IS NOT."

The location of this house was at 1635 Rancho Avenue, Glendale. Most of the shrubbery which grew on or next to the house is gone.

Across the street from Wilma Lentz's house is a park, now known as the Bette Davis Picnic Area.

"Sick people who couldn't wait to see me then suddenly were perfectly all right."

SKY TERRACE

The Sky Terrace nightclub/restaurant was located at the old San Fernando Valley Country Club. Now known as the Woodland Hills Country Club, it is located at 21150 Dumetz Road in Woodland Hills. The original buildings have been renovated and enlarged.

"Hey, Miles, when did you get back?"

"The boy says his father isn't his father and the woman says her sister isn't her sister."

"Well, this is the oddest thing I've ever heard of. Let's hope we don't catch it. I'd hate to wake up some morning and find out that you weren't you."

"What happened to the crowd tonight?"

Above, a 1944 aerial view of the Woodland Hills Country Club.
Below, vintage photographs of the club.

BELICEC HOME

The Belicec home was actually the garage/outbuilding on the old Chandler estate in the Los Feliz section of Los Angeles. The original entrance was located at 2330 Hillhurst Avenue, with a back entrance at 2411 Inverness Avenue. After the filming was completed, portions of the estate were subdivided. The back entrance is now the only entrance to the property.

"Emergency." "There's Jack."

"Well, you won't believe it, Miles, but you can see it for yourself."

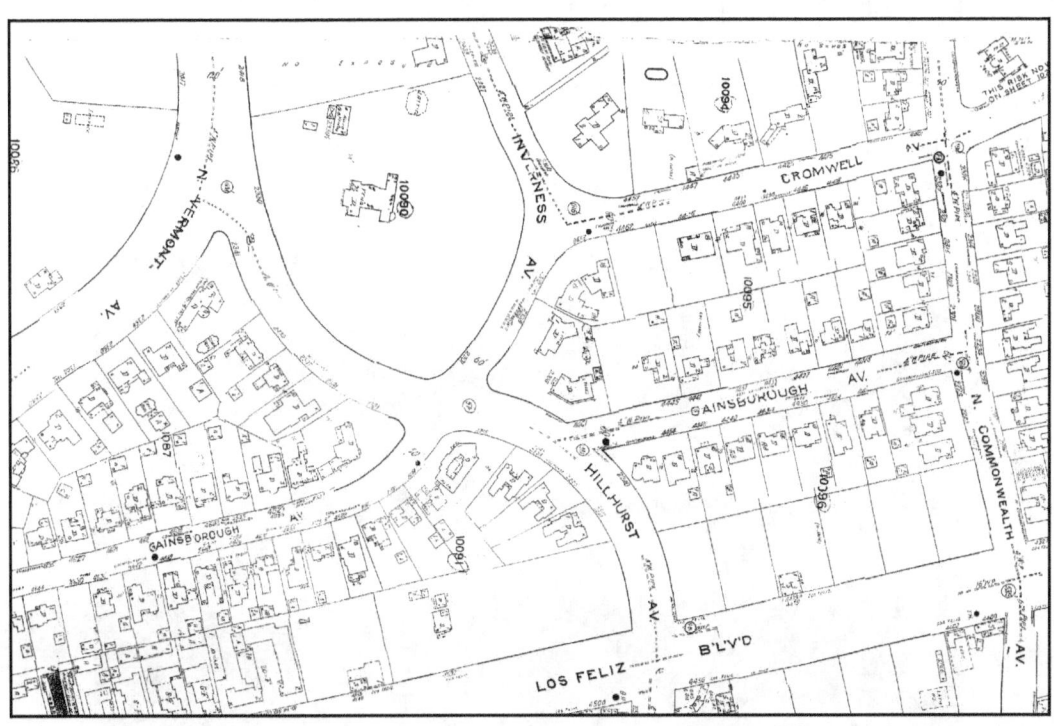

Above is a partial Sanborn Fire Insurance Map showing the Chandler Estate property between Hillhurst Avenue and Inverness Avenue.

Above is an historical aerial photograph of the Chandler Estate (circled in white). Below is a current aerial photograph of the area (looking towards the west).

BECKY DRISCOLL'S HOUSE

Becky Driscoll's house was located at 1927 Rodney Drive. It, along with all of the other houses on the block, are long gone, replaced with apartments.

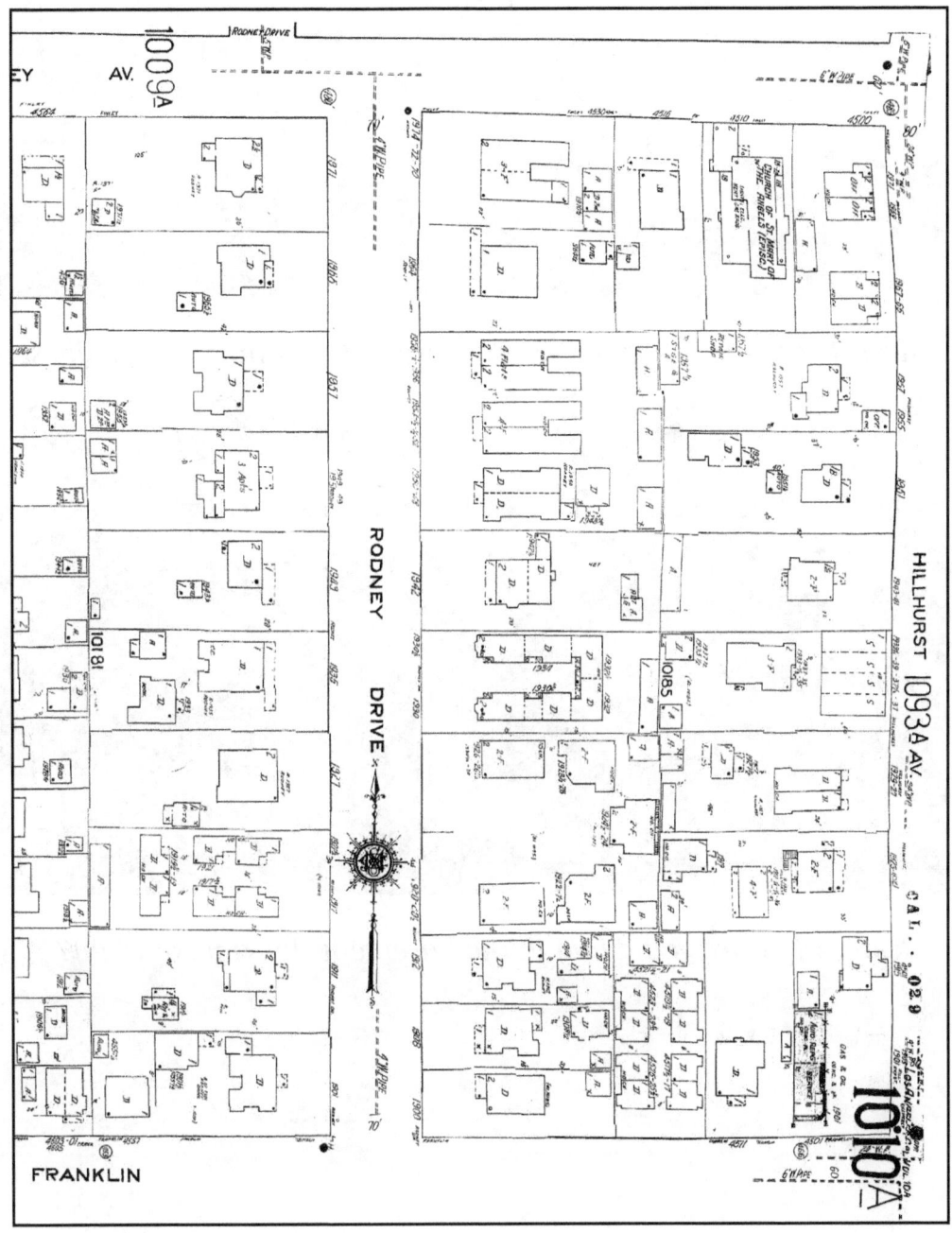

"I was careful not to let Becky know, but for the first time I was really scared."

"Dad, what are you doing in the basement this time of night?"

Above is the current location of Becky Driscoll's house. The buildings below were across the street from the house.

DR. MILES BENNELL'S HOUSE

There was no real exterior location utilized for Dr. Miles Bennell's house. All of the interior and exterior of the home was built on a sound stage at the Monogram/Allied Artists Studio.

Behind these walls of the old Monogram/Allied Artists Studio can be seen a portion of the first sound stage A and farther back to the right with the round opening or window is sound stage C (also used as a Process Stage).

BECKY DRISCOLL'S HOUSE

After a trip back to his own house, Miles returned to Becky's house.

"I was going to ring the bell, then I had a hunch I had better be careful."

"Becky! Becky! Becky!"

WILMA LENTZ'S ANTIQUE STORE

This building, which no longer exists, was located at 20 South Baldwin Avenue, Sierra Madre. It is now a parking lot for the market on the corner.

"Did you make that appointment for me with the psychiatrist?"

"Will you give Becky a call and tell her about it?"

"Becky's still at his house."

The building seen through the window of the store can be seen in the above aerial photograph in the upper left side of the street.

The above painting by Edna Lenz shows the building located at 20 S. Baldwin Avenue. Originally the home of Martin Olsen, a cobbler, who opened a shoe shop in 1887. Before being torn down in 1956 for an expansion of the market next door, the house had reportedly been used as a print shop, a Red Cross Headquarters, the residence of Orson Wells, a mortuary, and finally as the Le Grifon Antique Shop as it appeared in **Invasion of the Body Snatchers**.

DR. MILES BENNELL'S OFFICE

The interior of Dr. Miles Bennell's office (the two room and closet set) was located on a Monogram/Allied Artist Studio sound stage. The lobby card below shows a portion of that set.

LOMAX GAS STATION

The gas station used for the Lomax Gas Station was located at 1200 N. Virgil Avenue, on the northeast corner of Virgil Avenue and Lexington Avenue. The station is long gone.

"Listen, will you give me a couple of gallons fast? I'm in a hurry."

"I saw Mac closing the trunk of my car."

"What's the matter?"

The Lomas Gas Station was located on the corner of Virgil Avenue and Lexington Avenue. When Miles departed the station, he drove down Virgil Avenue and turned west onto Lexington Avenue, headed for the alley halfway down the street. Below is a now photo of the same scene above.

"We've got to make it to Sally's house."

SALLY WITHER'S HOUSE

The house used for Sally Wither's was located at 4400 Russell Street, Los Angeles. It is still there, but the side of the house is covered by heavy shrubbery and is not easy to see. The front is still fairly open to view.

"I wasn't sure now there was anyone I could trust, but I took a chance and drove to Sally's anyway."

"When I saw several cars in front of the house, I decided to play it safe."

"Becky, get going!"

Above, a current view of the front of the house. Below, an aerial view of the house (corner of Commonwealth Avenue and Russell Avenue).

STOCK FOOTAGE

At this point in the movie, between the fleeing from Sally's house and the entering of the alley behind Miles' office, the final shooting script does not include the police car montage. It does contain a scene, later cut, which has Becky stating that no one was following them. In an earlier script, there was to be a scene of Miles and Becky attempting to escape from the city only to find the road blocked. After the film was completed, it was decided to include the montage police car scenes in place of the scripted scene(s). None of these montage scenes were filmed for **Invasion of the Body Snatchers**. It appears that the scenes were from two other and different films based on the police cars.

The Hot Dog Show was located at 4300 W. Riverside Drive, Burbank. This scene was inserted into Invasion from some other movie after principal filming had taken place. It replaced already lensed scenes which were cut to expedite this portion of the film. It is not considered one of the locations of Invasion.

The Chevron Station was located at S. LaBrea Ave and Third Street. The Majestic Upholstering Co. address was 265 S. LaBrea Ave. Again, this scene was not shot for Invasion but for some other prior movie.

This location also was not filmed for Invasion but for some other movie. This was the Bill Dawson Service at 4405 W. Riverside Drive, Burbank.

The Gilmore Gas Station located at Third Street and Fairfax Avenue, near the Farmer's Market, was used in this stock footage.

THE ALLEY

To the east of 1710 N. Vermont Avenue, behind the frontage buildings, is an alley, between Kingswell Avenue to the north and Prospect Avenue to the south. The parking lot seen in the film as a used car lot, is still there. The house to the north of it has become another parking lot.

"We'll try to make my office. Cut in to that alley on the right."

In the below image, on the left on the building can be seen the last 4 letters of the word "Pastry". This building housed Sarno's Pastry and Pizzeria, its wares sold in the store front facing Vermont Avenue, with an entrance next to the doorway to the stairs heading to the second floor.

The historical aerial photograph to the left was shot about the time of the filming of the movie. Enclosed in white lines are the bakery/office building with the stairs in the rear (right side) and the parking lot.

Sarnos Pastry and Sarnos Pizzeria are both gone. Begun in 1946, they lasted until the year 2000. While growing up in the 1950-60s there, I had a friend who lived on the second floor with his sister and parents. The parents worked for the Sarnos downstairs.

The aerial photograph to the left is a current view of the same area. The back bakery area of the building has been transformed into a restaurant.

THE STAIRWAY AT THE REAR OF DR. MILES BENNELL'S OFFICE

Located at 1710 N. Vermont Avenue, at the rear of the building, facing the alleyway, was a wooden stairway which lead up from the parking area to the second floor. Sometime after 1963, the wooden stairway was removed and a metal one installed.

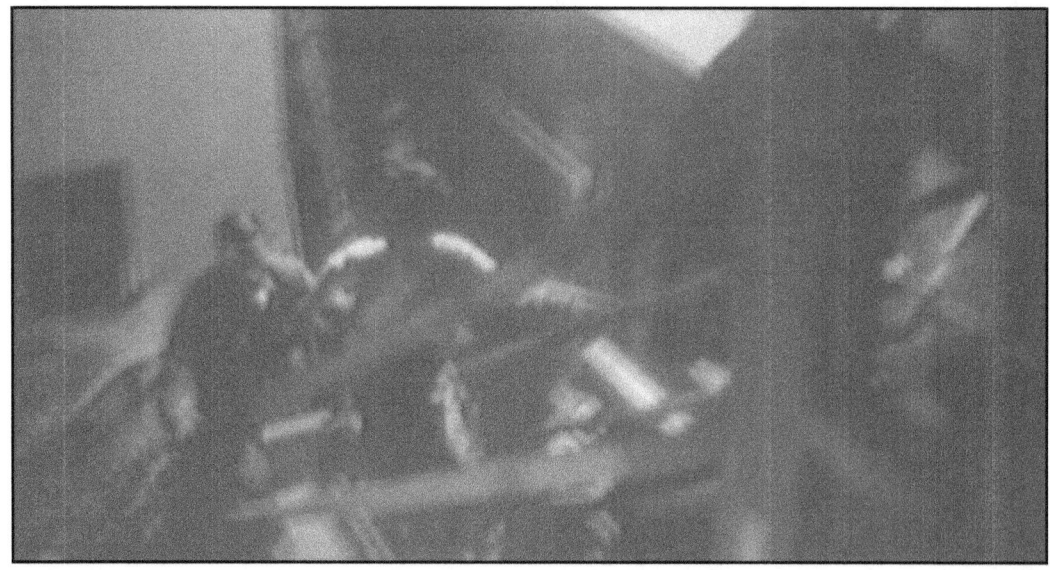

Two views of the back stairs during the 1980's and 1990's.

DR. MILES BENNELL'S OFFICE HALLWAY

The actual interior hallway to the second floor of 1710 N. Vermont Avenue was utilized for filming purposes, from the back door to the alley stairway, to the front entrance on Vermont Avenue.

Above is the hallway from the rear of the building to the front. Below you can see the front hallway, running parallel to the street.

In the below image, are the stairs leading out to Vermont Avenue. Notice that the transom over the door is rectangular. Then compare it to the transom over the door from the exterior side, as filmed in Sierra Madre. It has a half-moon shape.

SANTA MIRA TOWN SQUARE

The center of Sierra Madre stood in for the city of Santa Mira. This triangular area is located at Sierra Madre Boulevard, Baldwin Avenue, and Kersting Court.

"Just like any Saturday morning."

"There's the answer ... must be strangers in town."

"If you have Crescent City families, step over to truck number one."

Above is a ground level view of the Sierra Madre/Santa Mira town center. Below is an aerial view, looking south, which includes this same triangular area in the left bottom side of the photograph.

Compare the windows above the doorway in these two frames of film. Above is the exterior in Sierra Madre. Below is the interior side in Los Angeles. Above has divided panes. Below has a solid piece of glass.

THE CHASE

Miles and Becky begin running from Sierra Madre. The next time we seen them in their rush to escape Santa Mira is at the intersection of Beachwood Drive, Belden Drive, and Westshire drive as they run through the Richfield Gas Station lot (Richfield is the former name for Atlantic Richfield/ARCO). The station is no longer there.

"I'm sorry, Miles."

Miles and Beck being chased up Westshire Drive from Beachwood Drive.

"Here, the steps!"

The bottom end of the stairs is located between 2744 and 2748 Westshire Drive.

"There's only a few steps more!"

The top of the stairs are between 2823 and 2831 Hollyridge Drive, just north of Pelham Place.

An aerial view looking west of Beachwood Drive, Belden Drive, and Westshire Drive.

An aerial view looking east showing the location, hidden, of the stairway from Westshire Drive up to Hollyridge Drive near Pelham Place.

They race across Hollyridge Drive and head down the hillside, located between the present addresses of 2823 and 2831 Hollyridge Drive. The homes on the east side of the street did not exist at the time of the filming.

Above, the house next to the right of the top of the stairs. Below, the house blocking the view, across the street from the stairs.

The entrance to the Bronson Canyon Cave area can be seen in the distance to the right of Becky, as seen from the east side of Hollyridge Drive.

In the aerial photograph below, the arrow on the left indicates their approximate location on Hollyridge Drive. The arrow on the right shows the Bronson Canyon Cave area as seen in the above frame.

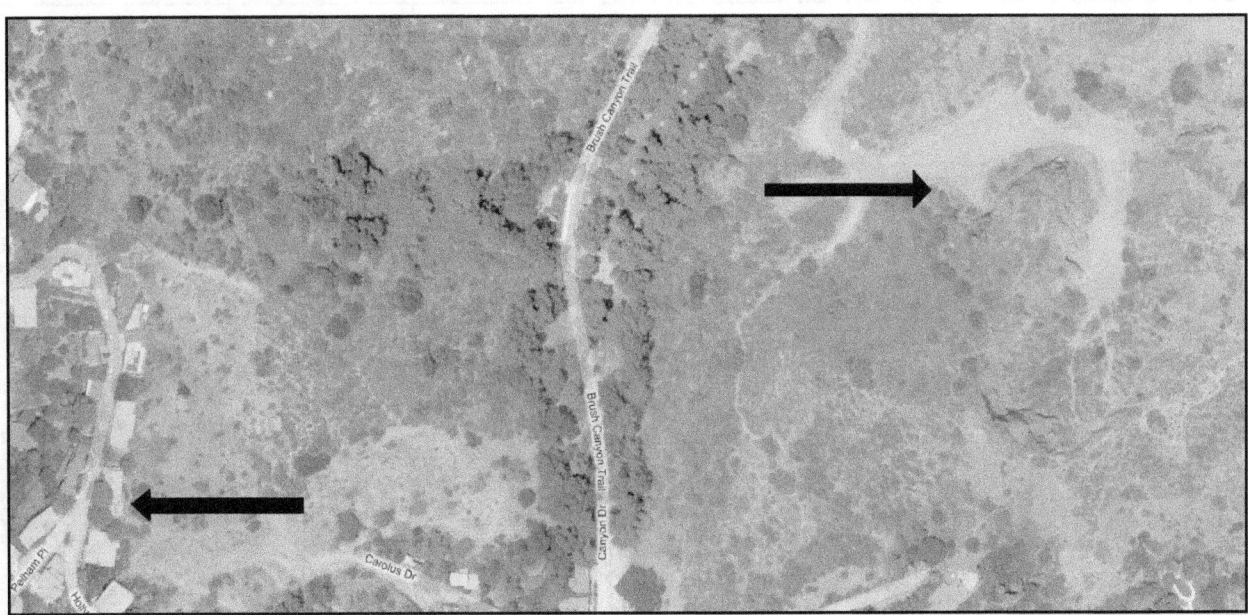

BRONSON CANYON

The famous cave scene in which Becky Driscoll is transformed into a pod person was filmed at the Bronson Canyon Caves. They are located at the north end of Canyon Drive, where there is a parking lot. Follow the dirt road on the west side of the street until you reach the cave area.

Above, looking west, as they run towards the cave. Below, same view, but from inside the west cave entrance.

The above photo shows the entrance area, from a slightly more northerly position. A few homes on the east side of Hollyridge Drive can be seen in the distance. Below is a modern-day view from the inside of the cave, looking westward.

"I never heard anything so beautiful."

The east side of the Bronson Canyon caves has three openings which branch off from the one western opening. The southern most opening was used in the film.

THE POD FARM

The pod farm was located at the old Goya Nursery in Sierra Madre, then located at 600 Wilcox Street (now known as Sierra Meadow Drive). The nursery no longer exists.

"This is Station KCAA—the twenty-four hour platter parade—the station of music."

Above is a 1954 aerial photograph of the Goya Nursery (in the white rectangle). Below is the same area as the nursery in a current aerial photograph.

BRONSON CANYON

Returning to the cave, Miles discovers that Becky has become a pod person. He escapes from the cave and is chased by the Body Snatchers.

"Kaufman and all the rest. Their bodies were now hosts harboring an alien ..."

"...form of life...a cosmic form...which to survive must take over every human man."

65

These two current photographs duplicate the filming areas as seen on the previous page.

MULHOLLAND DRIVE

The final exterior location in the film was Mulholland Drive, in and crossing the Hollywood Freeway. The hill which Miles and the pod people come down is west of the freeway, a quarter mile along Mulholland. Miles ran down the road (headed north) towards the bridge, and emoted his final exterior scenes on the bridge.

"I ran as little Jimmy Grimaldi had run the other day."

Left: A current photo of the location in the above image.

"My only hope was to get away from Santa Mira, to get to the highway."

Miles ran down this road, Mulholland Drive, from the area to the right of the FedEx truck to where I am standing at the bridge behind me and to my left. The left arrow below shows the hill exit location and the right arrow show the direction of Miles' run towards the bridge over the freeway.

The final exterior scenes of the film were performed on the Mulholland Drive bridge over the Hollywood Freeway. Above is an aerial view, looking southeast. The right most part of the bridge is the area seen in the below photograph, the area where Miles entered the bridge.

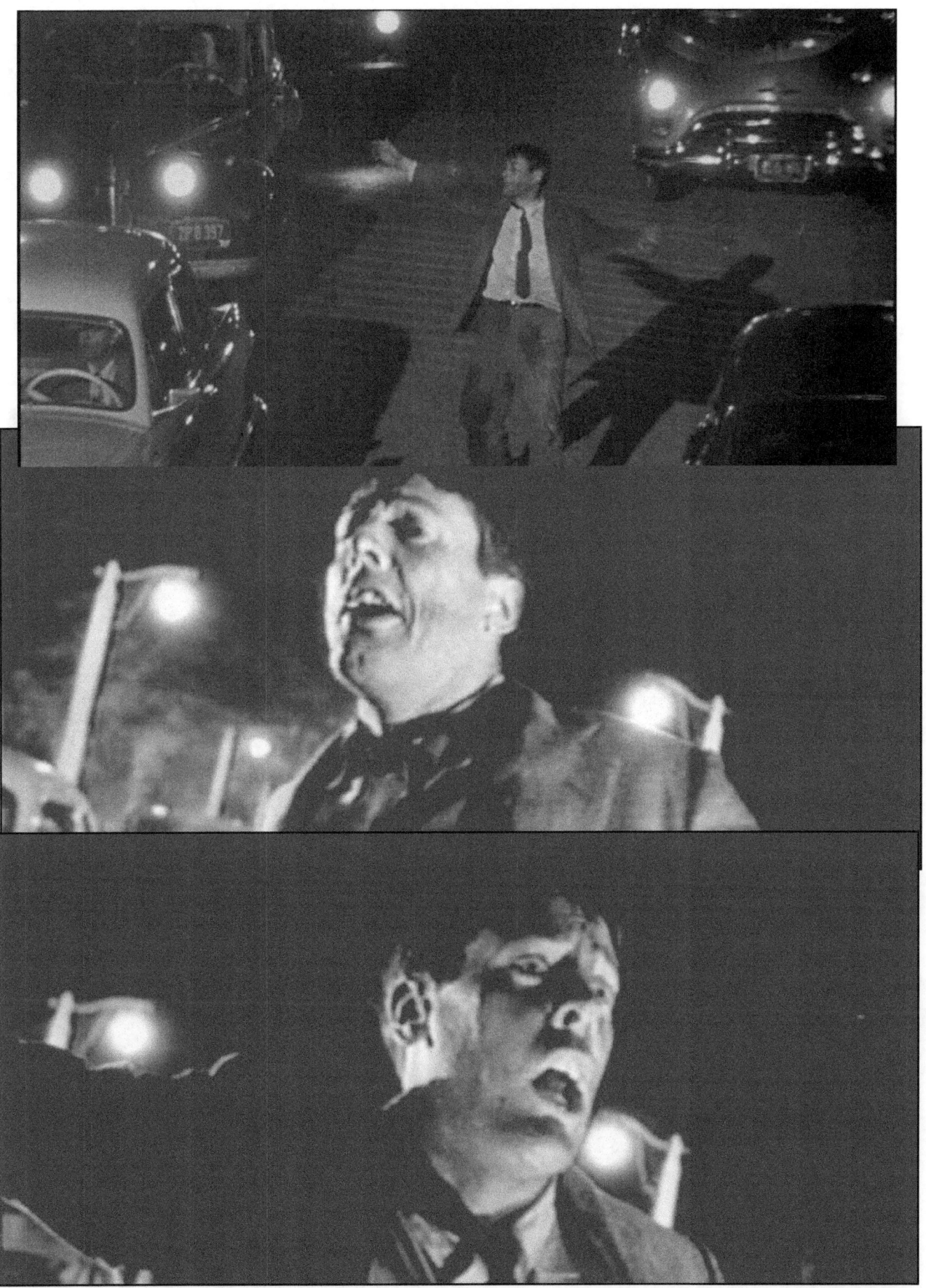

"You're next! You're next!

YOU'RE NEXT! YOU'RE NEXT!"

THE HOSPITAL

The final scenes at the hospital were shot at the Monogram/Allied Artists Studio.

*"Operator, get me the
Federal Bureau of Investigation!
Yes, it's an emergency."*

AFTERWORD

I spent my early years of life in the East Hollywood area of California near the intersection of Hollywood Boulevard and Vermont Avenue. During 7th grade, many days I passed by the old Monogram/Allied Artists Studio on my way home from school. The alley I played in and traveled through virtually every day of my youth was the same alley used for the back entrance to Dr. Miles Bennell's office. In fact, I had a friend who lived in the back portion of the second story of the building, the same floor where Dr. Miles' office was located, and where I played several times. The entrance to my friend's apartment can be seen in the film.

Some of the locations I discovered either by accident or because a movie still of the film showed the actual street sign in the background. However, I had only discovered less than half of the filming sites (or knew where they were) before I learned that the State Historical Society of Wisconsin Library in Madison, Wisconsin, contained the Walter Wanger Archives. In those archives are three versions of the script. But it is the third version, identified as the "Final Revised 3/17/55", that contained a page with ALL of the filming locations, addresses, and contacts.

Even though I now had the address of the Goya Nursery in Sierra Madre, location of the Pod Farm in the film, the address for the business and the business itself no longer existed. Last year I discovered a mention of the nursery in a Pasadena newspaper and its location in relationship to another place (the famous Wisteria vine house). Then, I discovered the Historic Aerial website. Using a 1954 aerial of Sierra Madre, along with the approximate street location, I found the long elusive Nursery.

I gratefully acknowledge the kind and generous assistance of Melissa R. Janz, Reference Assistant at the State Historical Society of Wisconsin, without whose help this book would not be complete.

I also have made extensive use of the book "Invasion of the Body Snatchers" by Don Siegel, director, Al LaValley, editor (Rutgers University Press, 1989).

THE PRODUCTION

Originally, producer Walter Wanger and director Don Siegel envisioned filming *Invasion of the Body Snatchers* on location in Jack Finney's (the author of the original story) model for Santa Mira, Mill Valley, just north of San Francisco. The location proved to be too costly, so only Los Angeles County locations were used.

Don Siegel and Walter Wanger

The film was originally budgeted for a 24-day shooting schedule at $454,864. However, studio requested that Wanger cut the budget to a 20-day shooting schedule at $350,000.

The film was shot in 23 days between March 23, 1955 and April 18, 1955 on a six-day workweek. The production went over schedule by three days, mainly because of night-for-night shooting. The final budget was $382,190.

The original cut of the film was to have Dr. Miles Bennell screaming hysterically as truckloads of pods pass him by. The studio insisted on adding a prologue and epilogue to the movie that suggested a more optimistic outcome to the story which is thus told mainly in flashback. In this final version of the film, it begins with Bennell in a hospital emergency room. He relates his story to a psychiatrist in flashback. The screenwriter scripted this framing story and Siegel shot it on September 16, 1955 at Allied Artists Studio.

The final cut of the film was seen by Wanger in December 1955 and he protested the use of the Superscope format. The film had been shot in the 1.85:1 aspect ratio, but the Superscope format stretched the film frame optically to mimic the Cinemascope format. Because of this, Wanger felt that the film lost sharpness and detail.

The film was copyrighted in 1955 by Allied Artists Pictures Corporation. When the studio declared bankruptcy, the film library was purchased by Lorimar. Lorimar was then bought out by Warner Bros., which, in turn, merged with Time Inc., creating the current Time-Warner. The only copyright renewal on record was by National Telefilm Assoc (NTA). However, there is no record of them obtaining a copyright transfer from either Allied Artists or Lorimar. Hence, it is believed that the film is in the public domain.

PHOTO GALLERY

Running for their life, not in the Hollywood Hills, nor a Los Angeles alley, but on the property of the Allied Artists Studio

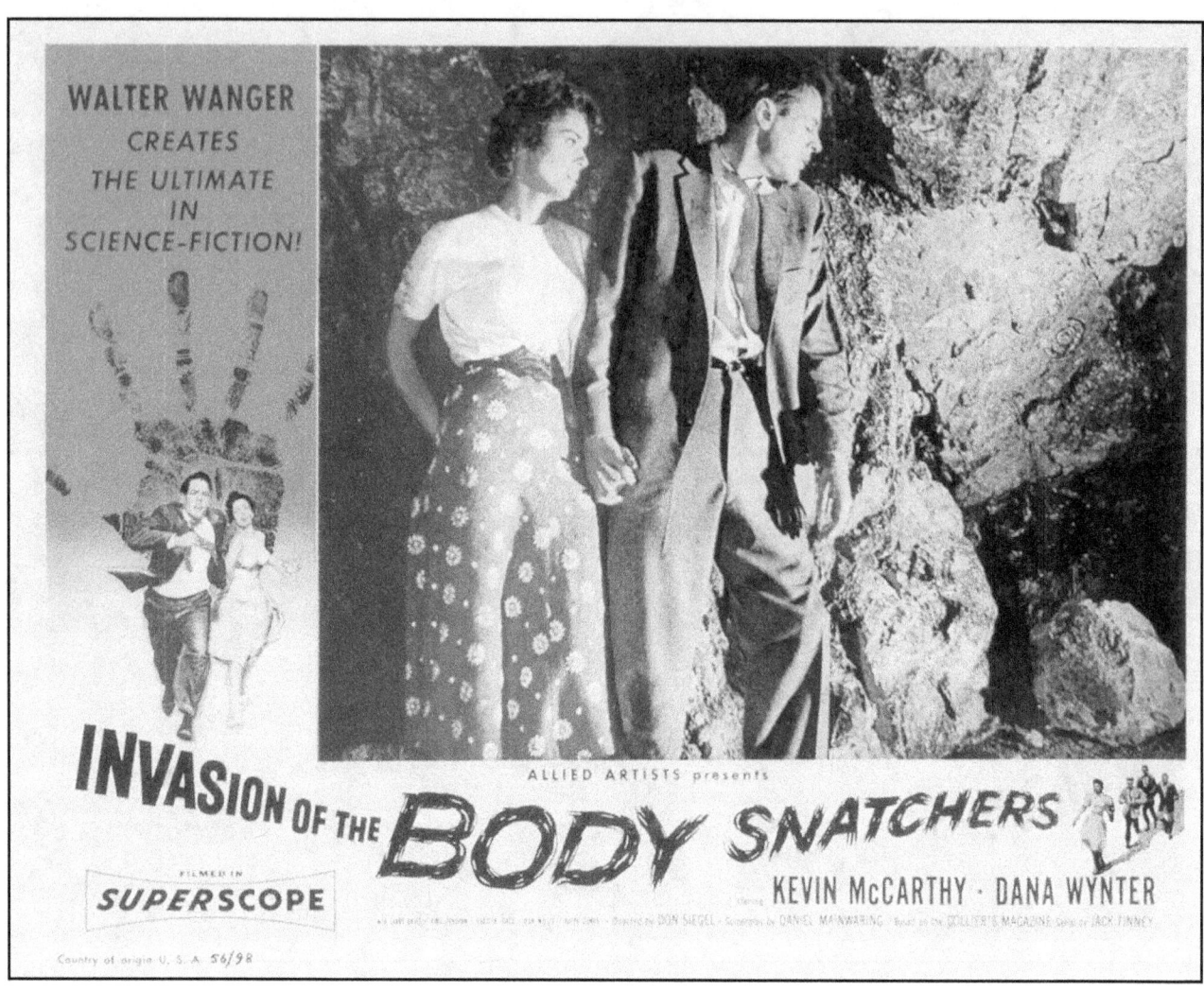

In the Bronson Canyon Cave

In Dr. Bennell's office, awaiting their fate.

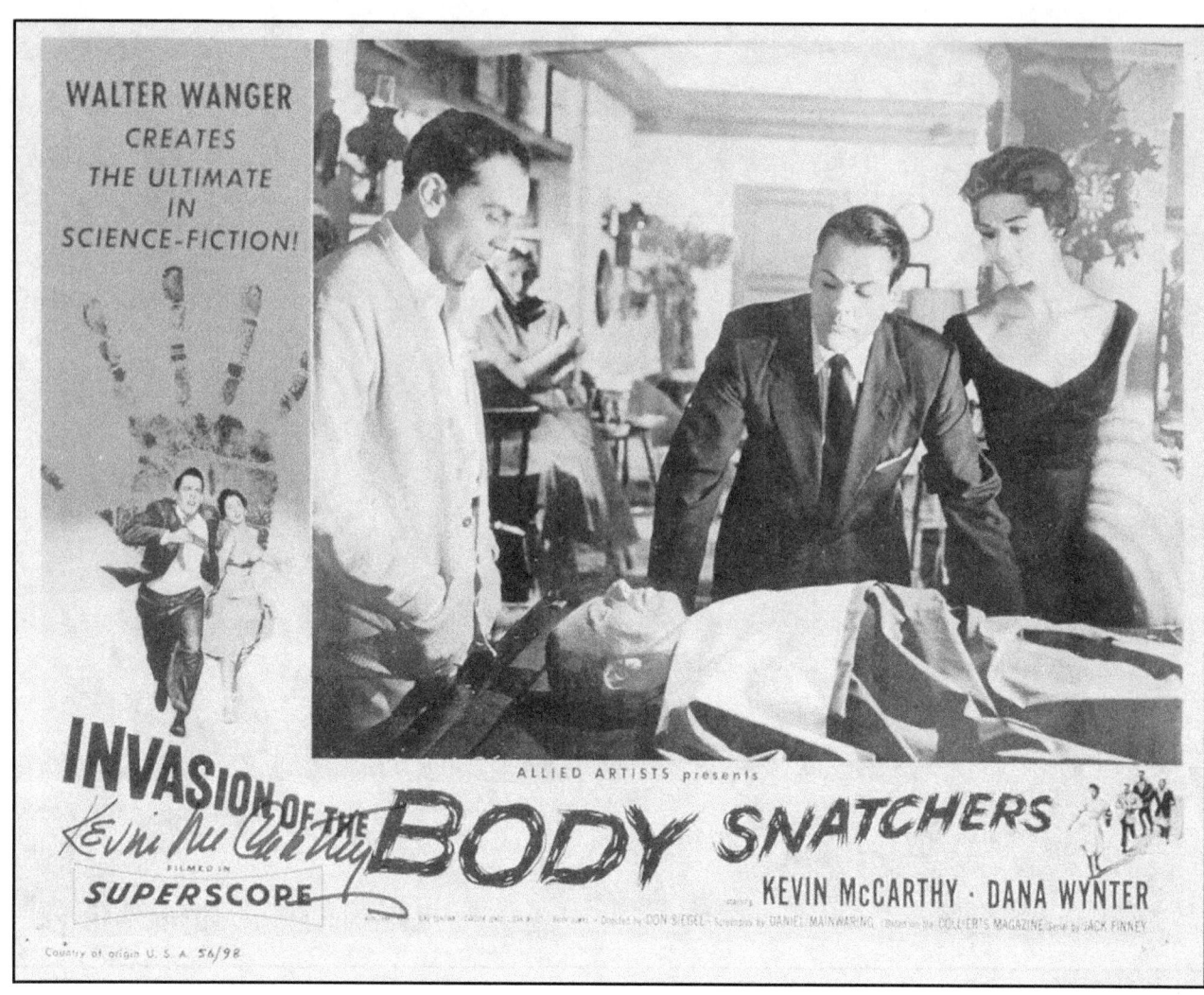

Jack's double at the Belicec home.

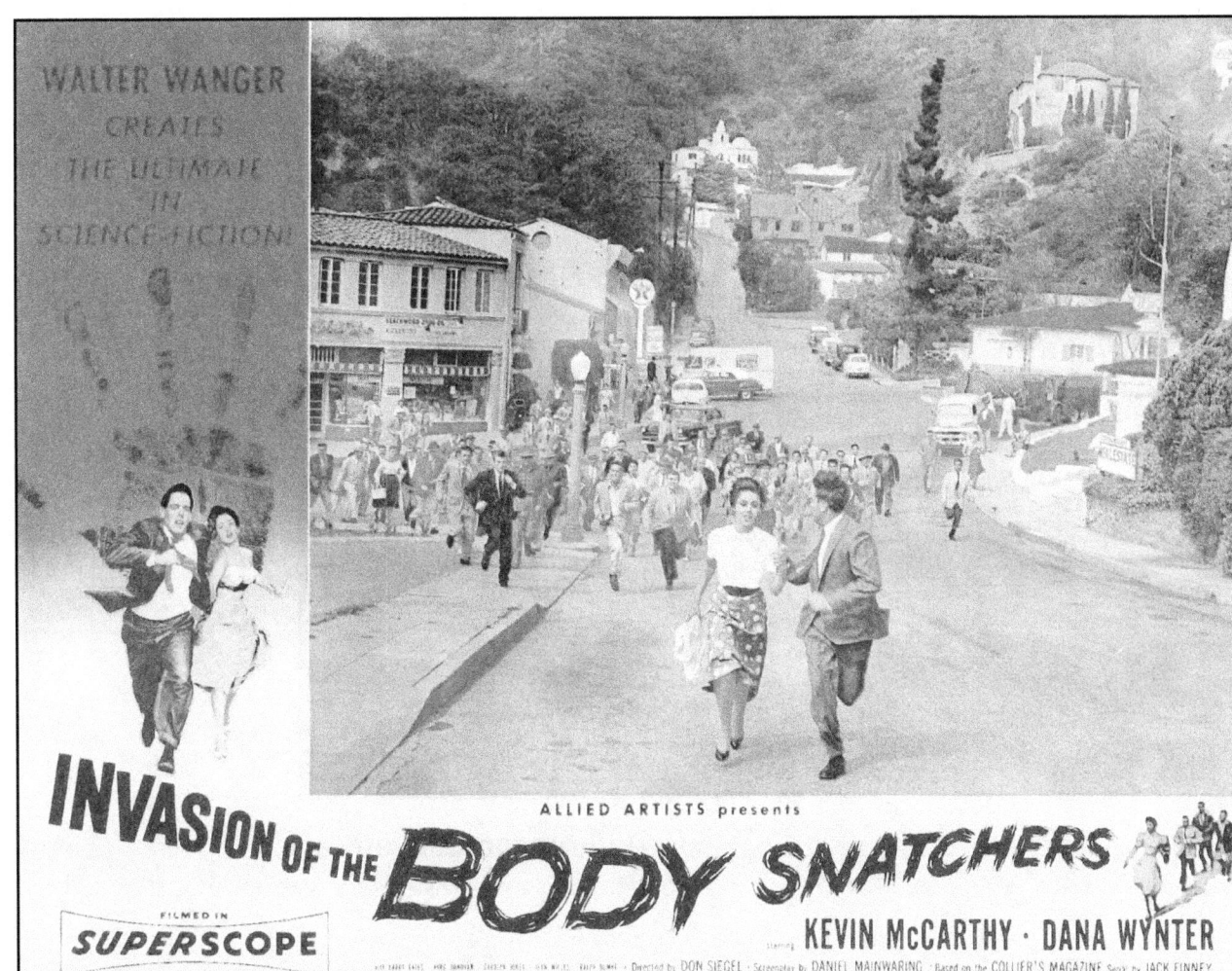

In Bronson Canyon cave.

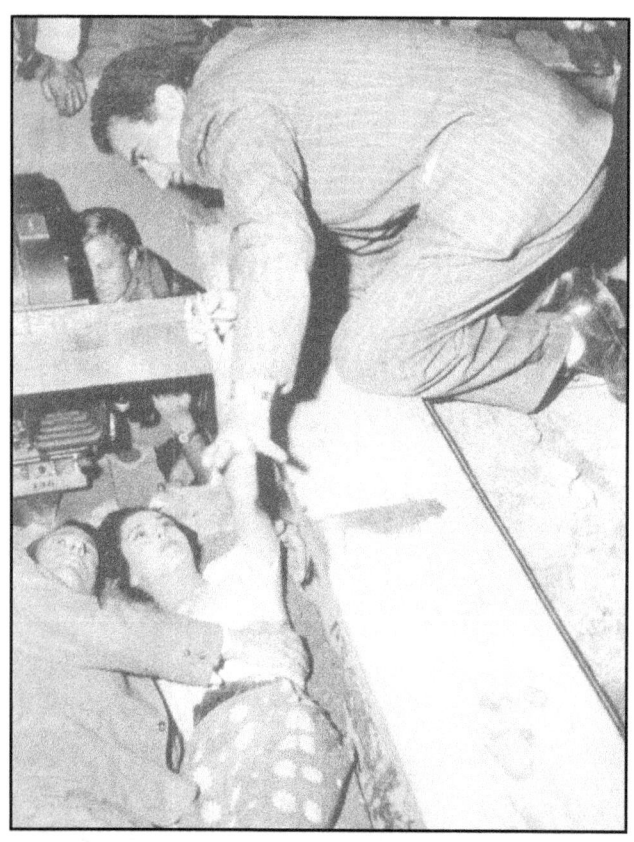

Preparing an underground shot with director Don Siegel. The location for this scene was not at Bronson Caves, but actually used a set on a sound stage on the Allied Artists lot.

Above, learning about the pod.

Below, "They're here!"

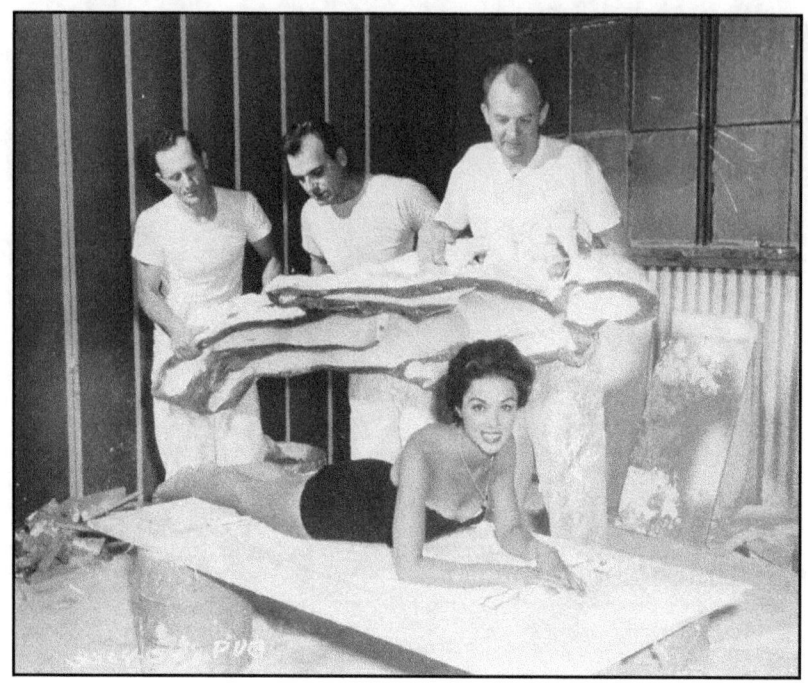

Above, a pod cast of Dana Wynter.

```
                    WALTER WANGER
                    ALLIED ARTISTS
                     4376 SUNSET DRIVE
                   LOS ANGELES 27, CALIFORNIA

                     April 20, 1955.


    Dear Emile,
              Thank you very much
    for the wonderful job you did on "THE
    BODY SNATCHERS".

              I assure you I enjoyed
    having you with us and trust the picture
    will be a success and we will soon be
    making another.

              Kindest regards,


                    WALTER F WANGER




    Mr. Emile LaVigne,
    Allied Artists Studios.
```

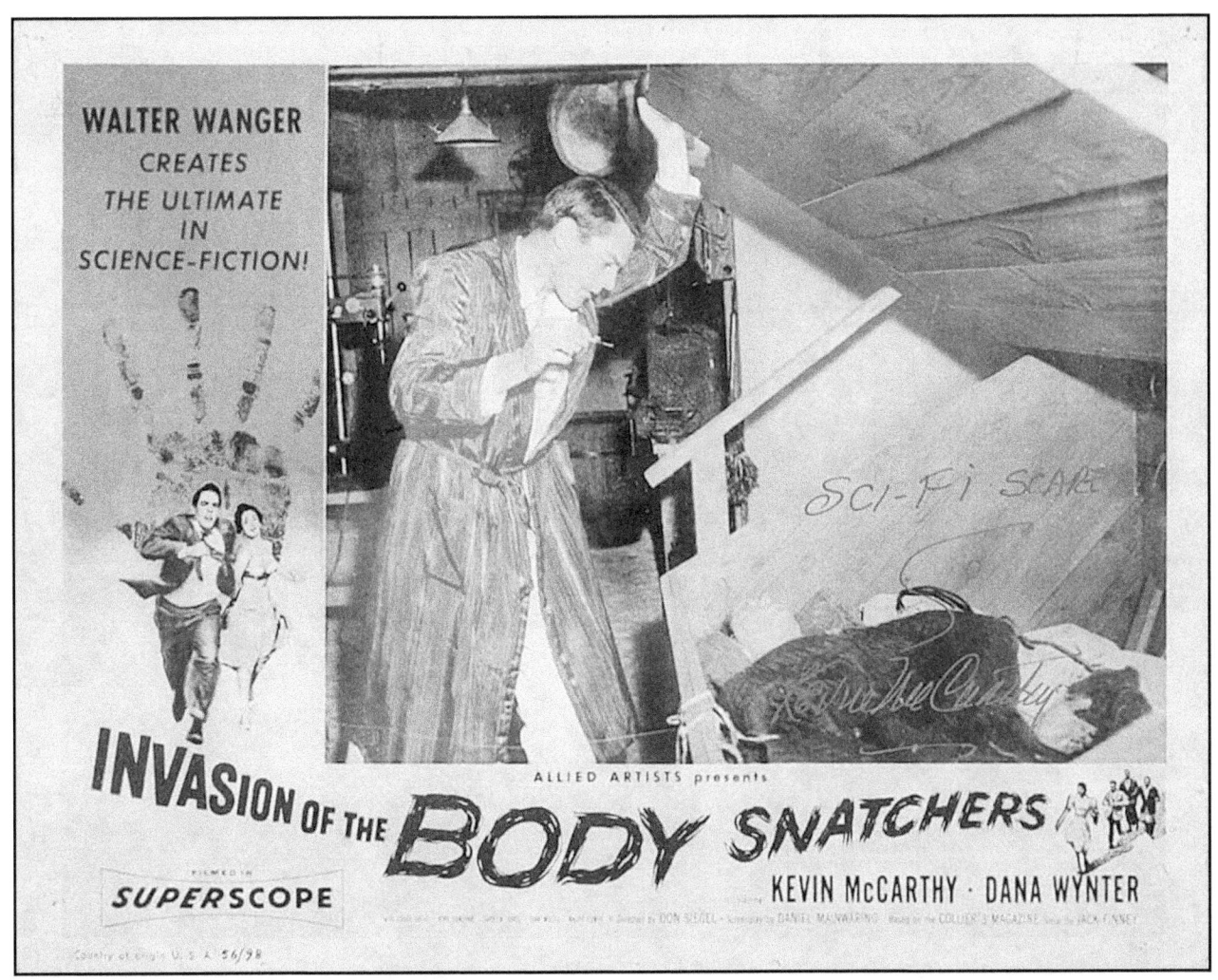

A pod discovered in Becky's house.

A historical view of Hollywoodland where the chase scenes began. The arrows show the location of the staircase ascended in the film. The "X" is at the intersection of Beachwood Drive, Belden Drive, and Westshire Drive.

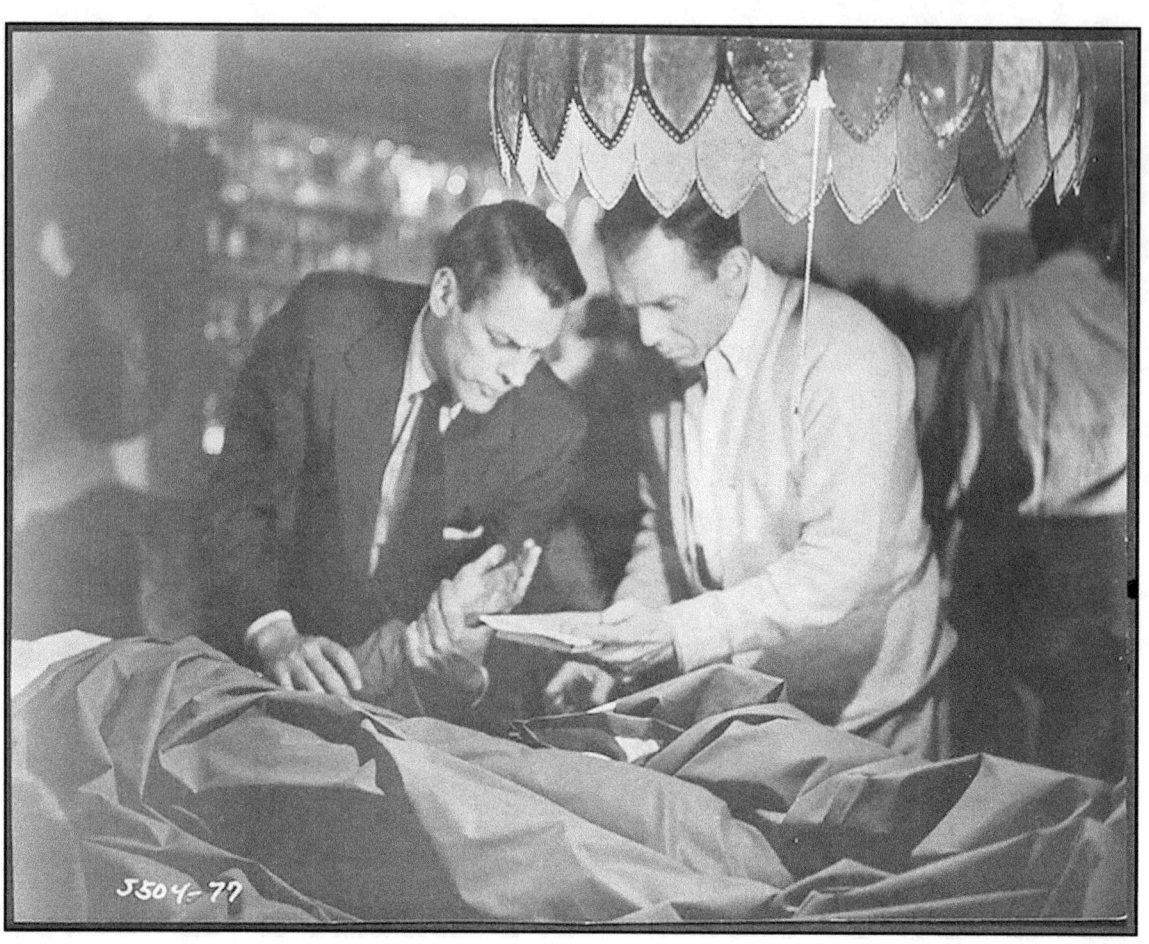

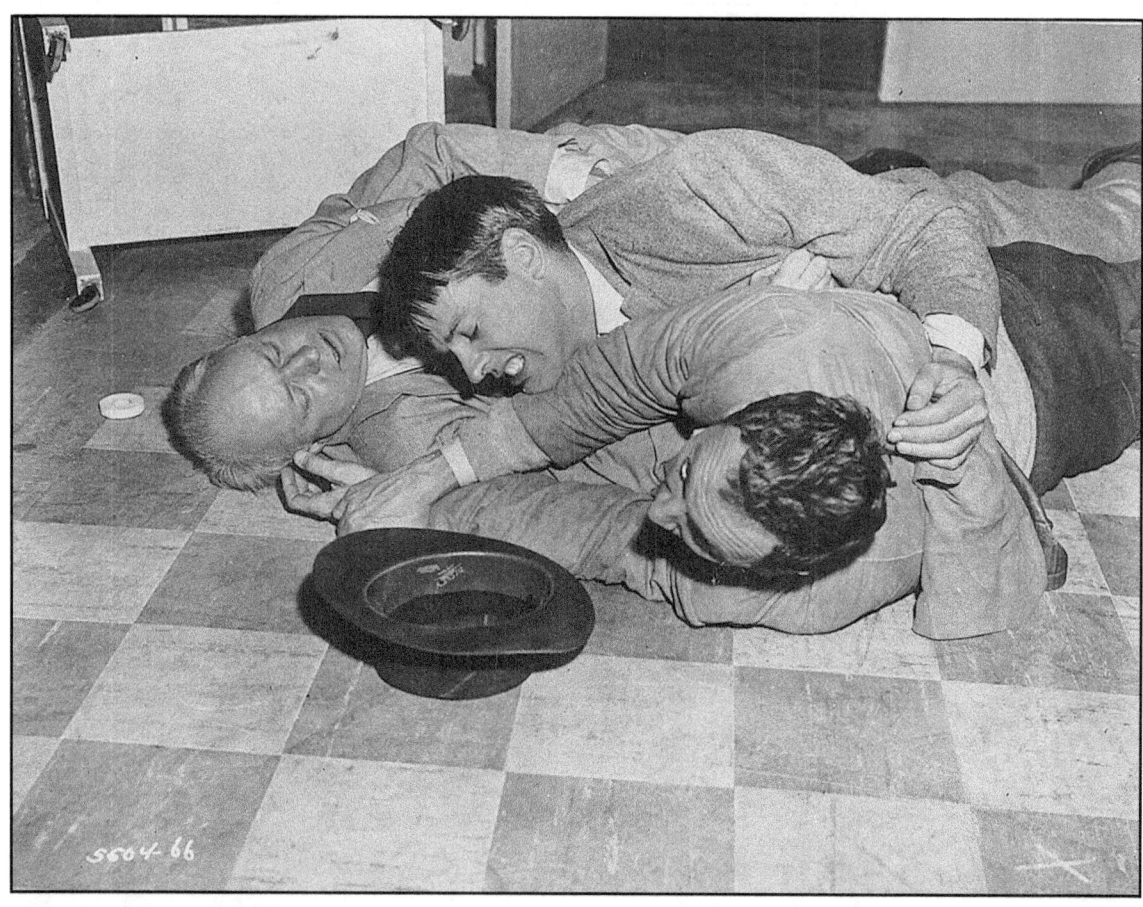

Collier's MAGAZINE CALLED IT...

The NIGHTMARE THAT THREATENS THE WORLD!

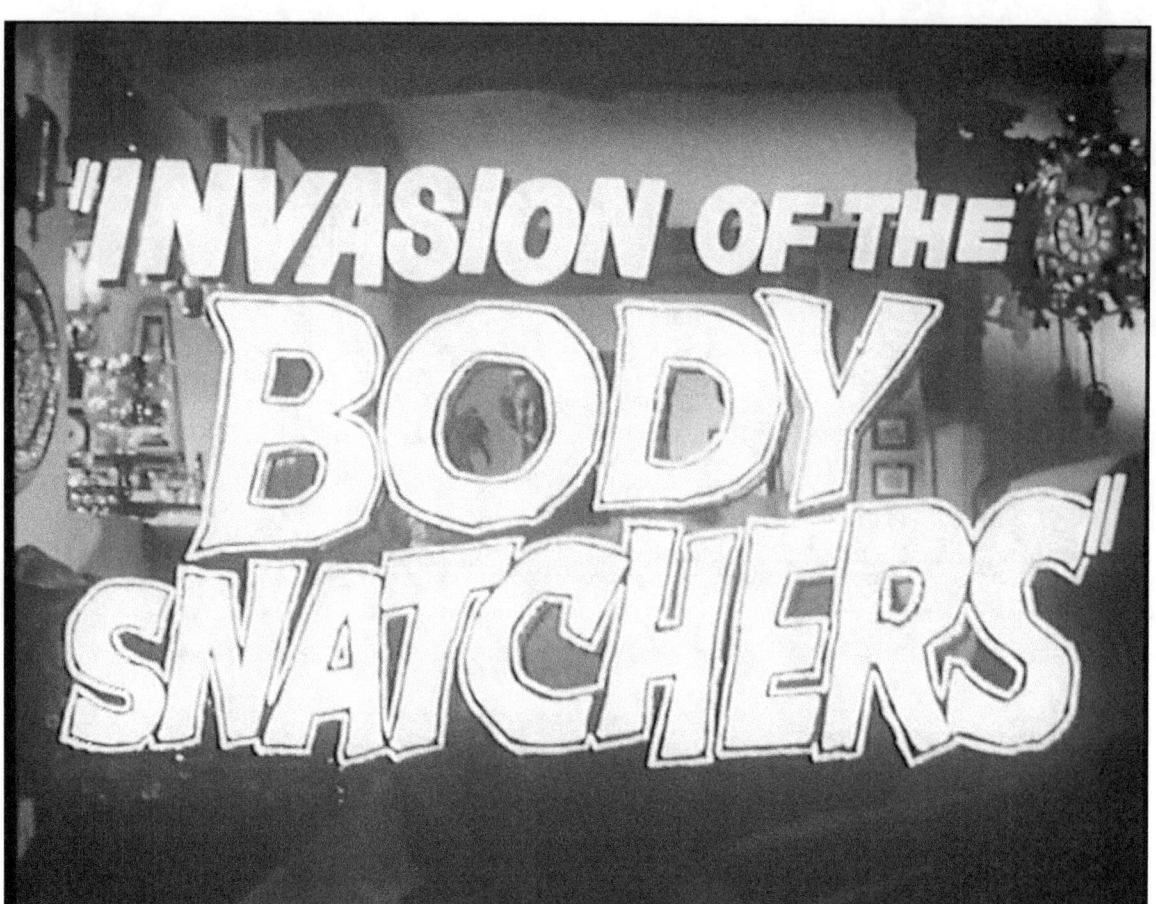

"INVASION OF THE BODY SNATCHERS"

IN SUPERSCOPE · AN ALLIED ARTISTS PICTURE

TO THE READER

TO THE reading lover, an interesting, entertaining book is a bargain at any price—their problem being one of finding the right book to suit their personal taste—the kind of story that offers the most reading enjoyment.

Variety is essential to reading pleasure. And the publishers of **CP ENTERTAINMENT BOOKS** make every effort to provide the widest possible selection for the discriminating reader.

Under the **CP ENTERTAINMENT BOOKS** imprint appear biographies, pop culture, art, photography, genealogy, mystic, religion, reference, and performing arts—entertaining escape from the everyday world.

You will always find your greatest reading satisfaction under the distinctive imprint of **CP ENTERTAINMENT BOOKS**.

Find the **CP Entertainment Books** online at:

www.FictionHousePress.com

www.ingramcontent.com/pod-product-compliance
Lightning Source LLC
Chambersburg PA
CBHW081204240426
43669CB00039B/2803